*Congressional
Research
Service*

Budget Control Act: Potential Impact of Sequestration on Health Reform Spending

C. Stephen Redhead
Specialist in Health Policy

October 1, 2012

Congressional Research Service

7-5700

www.crs.gov

R42051

CRS Report for Congress
Prepared for Members and Committees of Congress

Summary

The Budget Control Act of 2011 (BCA; P.L. 112-25) established new budget enforcement mechanisms for reducing the federal deficit by at least $2.1 trillion over the 10-year period FY2012-FY2021. The BCA placed statutory limits, or caps, on discretionary spending for each of those 10 fiscal years, which will save an estimated $0.9 trillion during that period. In addition, it created a Joint Select Committee on Deficit Reduction (Joint Committee) with instructions to develop legislation to reduce the federal deficit by at least another $1.5 trillion through FY2021. On November 21, 2011, the Joint Committee announced that it was unable to agree on a legislative package of deficit cuts, which raises the likelihood of automatic annual spending reductions beginning in FY2013. Under the BCA, the reductions would be achieved by a combination of sequestration—an automatic across-the-board cancellation of budgetary resources (i.e., spending cuts) for nonexempt direct spending programs—and lowering the caps on discretionary spending.

The potential impact of spending reductions triggered by the BCA on health reform spending under the Patient Protection and Affordable Care Act (ACA) would appear to be somewhat limited. ACA sought to increase access to affordable health insurance by expanding the Medicaid program and by restructuring the private health insurance market. It set minimum standards for private insurance coverage, created a mandate for most U.S. residents to obtain coverage, and provided for the establishment by 2014 of state-based insurance exchanges for the purchase of health insurance. Certain individuals and families will be able to receive federal subsidies to reduce the cost of purchasing coverage through the exchanges. The new law included direct spending to subsidize the purchase of health insurance coverage through the exchanges, as well as increased outlays for the Medicaid expansion. Under the rules governing sequestration, Medicaid spending would be exempt from any reduction, and cuts to Medicare would be capped at 2%.

ACA also included numerous mandatory appropriations that provide billions of dollars to support temporary programs to increase coverage and funding for targeted groups, provide funds to states to plan and establish exchanges, and support many other research and demonstration programs and activities. These appropriations would, in general, be subject to direct spending reductions under a sequestration order. However, for any given fiscal year in which sequestration was ordered, only new budget authority for that year (including advance appropriations that first become available for obligation in that year) would be reduced. Unobligated balances carried over from previous fiscal years would be exempt from sequestration.

ACA is likely to affect discretionary spending subject to the annual appropriations process. The law reauthorized appropriations for numerous existing discretionary grant programs and activities authorized under the Public Health Service Act, permanently reauthorized funding for the Indian Health Service (IHS), and created a number of new grant programs and provided for each an authorization of appropriations. In addition, the Congressional Budget Office projected that both the Department of Health and Human Services and the Internal Revenue Service will incur substantial administrative costs to implement the policies and programs established by ACA. Those costs will have to be funded largely through the annual appropriations process. ACA-related discretionary spending would, in general, be subject to automatic spending reductions triggered by the BCA.

Contents

Tables

Contacts

Introduction

The Budget Control Act of 2011 (BCA), which was enacted on August 2, 2011,[1] was the product of negotiations between the President and Congress to raise the nation's debt ceiling and avoid the federal government reaching its borrowing limit. The BCA gave the President the authority to increase the debt limit by at least $2.1 trillion (and up to $2.4 trillion) in three installments, and established a process by which Congress could block the second and third installments by passing a joint resolution disapproving the debt limit increase.[2]

In addition, the BCA established a process for reducing the federal deficit by at least $2.1 trillion over the 10-year period FY2012-FY2021. First, the law placed enforceable limits, or caps, on discretionary spending for each of the next 10 fiscal years.[3] For FY2012 and FY2013, separate caps for security and nonsecurity spending will be in effect.[4] For each of the remaining eight fiscal years (i.e., FY2014-FY2021), a single cap will apply to total discretionary spending. The Congressional Budget Office (CBO) estimated that adhering to the discretionary spending limits, which grow by approximately 2% each year, will reduce federal spending by $917 billion between FY2012 and FY2021, compared to the projected level of spending if annual appropriations were to grow at the rate of inflation.[5]

Second, the BCA created a Joint Select Committee on Deficit Reduction (Joint Committee), composed of an equal number of Democrats and Republicans from the House and Senate. The Joint Committee was instructed to develop legislation to reduce the federal deficit by at least another $1.5 trillion through FY2021.[6] It had until November 23, 2011, to approve a bill and have it considered by the House and Senate under special procedures that prevent amendments and limit debate in both chambers. If, by January 15, 2012, Congress and the President failed to enact a Joint Committee bill reducing the deficit by an amount greater than $1.2 trillion over the period FY2012-FY2021, then automatic annual spending reductions would be triggered beginning in FY2013.

---

[1] P.L. 112-25, 125 Stat. 240. For a more detailed examination of all the provisions in the BCA, see CRS Report R41965, *The Budget Control Act of 2011*, by Bill Heniff Jr., Elizabeth Rybicki, and Shannon M. Mahan.

[2] The President has exercised this authority and raised the debt ceiling by a total of $2.1 trillion, from $14.294 trillion to $16.394 trillion. The initial $400 billion increase in the debt limit took effect immediately upon enactment of the BCA. The second increase of $500 billion became effective on September 22, 2011, after the Senate rejected a motion to proceed to consider a joint resolution of disapproval (S.J.Res. 25) by a vote of 45-52. Following the action taken by the Senate, the House passed its own disapproval resolution (H.J.Res. 77) by a vote of 232-186. The third (and final) increase in the debt limit of $1.2 trillion took effect on January 30, 2012, after the Senate once again rejected a motion to proceed to consider a joint resolution of disapproval (H.J.Res. 98) by a vote of 44-52. Prior to the Senate's vote, the House passed H.J.Res. 98 by a vote of 239-176.

[3] Discretionary spending refers to outlays from budget authority (i.e., the authority to incur financial obligations that result in government expenditures) that is provided in and controlled by the annual appropriations acts.

[4] Security spending comprises discretionary appropriations for the Department of Defense, the Department of Homeland Security, the Department of Veterans Affairs, and other related activities. Nonsecurity spending comprises all discretionary appropriations not included in the security category.

[5] U.S. Congressional Budget Office, *Analysis of Budget Control Act*, August 1, 2011, http://www.cbo.gov/ftpdocs/123xx/doc12357/BudgetControlActAug1.pdf.

[6] The BCA placed no specific policy restrictions or requirements on the Joint Committee. The committee could recommend changes in federal revenues, spending, or both.

On November 21, 2011, the co-chairs of the Joint Committee announced that the group had been unable to reach agreement on a legislative proposal to cut the deficit, raising the likelihood that automatic spending reductions will be triggered.[7] Under the BCA, the spending reductions would be equally divided between defense spending and all other spending (i.e., nondefense spending).[8] The amount of reduction required in each category would then be divided proportionately between discretionary spending and nonexempt direct (i.e., mandatory) spending.[9] The reductions would be achieved (1) by an automatic across-the-board cancellation of budgetary resources (i.e., spending cuts)—a process known as sequestration—for nonexempt direct spending programs over the FY2013-FY2021 period, and for nonexempt discretionary spending in FY2013; and (2) by lowering the annual caps on discretionary spending for FY2014-FY2021.

Health Reform Implementation

There is considerable interest in how automatic spending reductions triggered by the BCA would affect implementation of the Patient Protection and Affordable Care Act (ACA), the health reform law enacted in March 2010.[10] Among its many provisions, ACA restructures the private health insurance market, sets minimum standards for health coverage, and, beginning in 2014, will require most U.S. residents to obtain health insurance coverage or pay a penalty. The law provides for the establishment by 2014 of state-based health insurance exchanges for the purchase of private health insurance. Qualifying individuals and families will be able to receive federal subsidies to reduce the cost of purchasing coverage through the exchanges.

In addition to expanding private health insurance coverage, ACA, as enacted, requires state Medicaid programs to expand coverage to all eligible nonelderly, non-pregnant individuals under age 65 with incomes up to 133% of the federal poverty level (FPL). Under ACA, the federal government will initially cover 100% of the expansion costs, phasing down to 90% of the costs by 2020. Medicaid law allows the Secretary of Health and Human Services (HHS) to withhold existing federal Medicaid matching funds if states refuse to comply with the expansion. However, in *National Federation of Independent Business v. Sebelius*, the U.S. Supreme Court found that the Medicaid expansion violated the Constitution by threatening states with the loss of their existing federal Medicaid matching funds. The Court precluded the HHS Secretary from penalizing states that choose not to participate in the Medicaid expansion (see text box below).

ACA also amends the Medicare program in an effort to reduce the rate of its projected growth; imposes an excise tax on insurance plans found to have high premiums; and makes many other

---

[7] The Joint Committee's statement is at http://www.deficitreduction.gov/public/index.cfm/2011/11/statement-from-co-chairs-of-the-joint-select-committee-on-deficit-reduction.

[8] The annual discretionary spending caps for FY2012-FY2021 would be revised if automatic spending reductions were triggered. The overall discretionary spending limit for each fiscal year would remain unchanged, but that amount would be divided between defense discretionary spending and all other (i.e., nondefense) discretionary spending. See, also, footnote 25.

[9] Direct, or mandatory, spending generally refers to budget authority that is provided in laws other than the annual appropriations acts. Mandatory spending includes entitlement authority (e.g., Medicare, Social Security).

[10] ACA was signed into law on March 23, 2010 (P.L. 111-148, 124 Stat. 119). A week later, on March 30, 2010, the President signed the Health Care and Education Reconciliation Act (HCERA; P.L. 111-152, 124 Stat. 1029), which amended multiple health care and revenue provisions in ACA. Several other bills that were subsequently enacted during the 111th and 112th Congresses made more targeted changes to specific ACA provisions. All references to ACA in this report refer to the law as amended. Note that previous CRS reports on the Patient Protection and Affordable Care Act used the acronym PPACA to refer to the law. CRS is now using the more common acronym ACA.

changes to the tax code, Medicare, Medicaid, the Children's Health Insurance Program (CHIP), and other federal programs.

U.S. Supreme Court Decision on ACA (June 28, 2012)

In *National Federation of Independent Business v. Sebelius (NFIB)*, the Court ruled on the constitutionality of both the individual mandate, which requires most U.S. residents (beginning in 2014) to carry health insurance or pay a penalty, and the Medicaid expansion. The Court upheld the individual mandate as a constitutional exercise of Congress's authority to levy taxes. The penalty is to be paid by taxpayers when they file their tax returns and enforced by the Internal Revenue Service.

In a separate opinion, the Court found that compelling states to participate in the ACA Medicaid expansion—which the Court determined to be essentially a new program—or risk losing their existing federal Medicaid matching funds was coercive and unconstitutional under the Spending Clause and the Tenth Amendment. The Court's remedy for this constitutional violation was to prohibit HHS from penalizing states that choose not be participate in the expansion by withholding any federal matching funds for their existing Medicaid programs. However, if a state accepts the new ACA expansion funds (initially a 100% federal match), it must abide by all the expansion coverage rules.

Under *NFIB*, all other provisions of ACA remain fully intact and operative.

ACA is projected to have a significant impact on federal direct spending and revenues. The law includes direct spending to subsidize the purchase of health insurance coverage through the exchanges, as well as increased outlays for the expansion of state Medicaid programs. ACA also includes numerous mandatory appropriations to fund temporary programs to increase access and funding for targeted groups, provide funding to states to plan and establish exchanges, and support many other research and demonstration programs and activities. The costs of expanding public and private health insurance coverage and other spending are offset by revenues from new taxes and fees, and by savings from payment and health care delivery system reforms designed to slow the growth in spending on Medicare and other federal health care programs.

Implementing ACA also is likely to affect discretionary spending, which is provided in and controlled by annual appropriations acts. The law established numerous new grant programs and provided for each an authorization of appropriations. It also reauthorized appropriations for many existing grant programs. While the authorization of appropriations for most of these existing programs expired prior to ACA's enactment, typically they continued to receive an annual appropriation.

Report Roadmap

This report examines how automatic spending reductions triggered by the BCA would affect health reform implementation under ACA. The details of such a process would depend on the statutory interpretations and analysis of the Office of Management and Budget (OMB). Each year, OMB would be responsible for determining the proportional allocation of required cuts to discretionary and nonexempt direct spending in both the defense and nondefense categories. It would also have exclusive authority in applying the exemptions and special rules related to sequestration. On September 14, 2012, pursuant to a congressional mandate, OMB released a preliminary analysis of the impact of a BCA-triggered sequestration on FY2013 spending.[11]

---

[11] U.S. Office of Management and Budget, *OMB Report Pursuant to the Sequestration Transparency Act of 2012 (P.L. 112-155)*, http://www.whitehouse.gov/sites/default/files/omb/assets/legislative_reports/stareport.pdf.

The report is divided into two sections. The first section provides an overview of ACA and describes the budgetary effects of its insurance coverage and other key spending provisions, based on CBO's estimates of the impact of ACA implementation on federal direct spending and revenues. The second section briefly reviews sequestration under the BCA and, with reference to OMB's new analysis of FY2013 spending cuts, discusses which types of health reform spending would likely be subject to, or exempt from, those reductions. This product is periodically revised and updated to reflect important legislative and other developments.

Patient Protection and Affordable Care Act

The primary goal of ACA is to increase access to affordable health insurance for the millions of Americans without coverage and make health insurance more affordable for those already covered. In addition, ACA makes numerous changes in the way health care is financed, organized, and delivered. These provisions are intended to slow the growth in health care costs and improve the quality of care by aligning payment incentives to increase efficiency and achieve savings; organizing care delivery systems to promote accountable, patient-centered, and coordinated care; and establishing benchmarks for better health outcomes.

While most of the major provisions of the law do not take effect until 2014, some provisions are already in place, and others are being phased in over the next few years.

Coverage Expansions and Market Reforms Prior to 2014

ACA created several temporary programs to increase access and funding for targeted groups. They include (1) temporary high-risk pools for uninsured individuals with preexisting conditions; (2) a reinsurance program to reimburse employers for a portion of the health insurance claims' costs for their 55- to 64-year-old retirees; and (3) small business tax credits for small employers with fewer than 25 full-time equivalents (FTEs) and average annual wages below $50,000 that choose to offer health insurance.

In addition, several of ACA's private insurance market reforms have taken effect. Health plans may not impose lifetime limits on the dollar value of essential benefits, rescind coverage (except in cases of fraud), or deny coverage to children up to age 19 based on a preexisting condition. Also, young adults up to age 26 generally must be allowed to remain on their parents' plans. Finally, plans must cover recommended preventive services and immunizations without any cost-sharing.

Coverage Expansions and Market Reforms Beginning in 2014

The major expansion and reform provisions in ACA take effect in January 2014. States are expected to establish health insurance exchanges through which eligible individuals and small employers will be able to purchase coverage from private health insurance plans offering standardized benefit and cost-sharing packages. In 2017, states may allow larger employers to purchase health insurance through the exchanges, but are not required to do so. The HHS Secretary will establish exchanges in states that do not create their own approved exchange. Refundable tax credits will be available to individuals and families who enroll in exchange plans, provided their income is generally at or above 100% and does not exceed 400% of FPL, to help offset the cost of the insurance premiums. In addition, certain individuals and families receiving the premium credit will be eligible for a subsidy to lower their cost-sharing (i.e., out-of-pocket costs such as deductibles and co-pays).

ACA's market reforms are further expanded in 2014, with no annual limits on the dollar value of essential benefits and no exclusions for preexisting conditions allowed regardless of age. Plans offered within the exchanges and certain other plans must meet essential benefit standards, requiring them to cover emergency services, hospital care, physician services, preventive care, prescription drugs, and mental health and substance use disorder treatment, among other specified services. Premiums may vary by limited amounts, but only based on age, family size, geographic area, and tobacco use. Finally, plans must sell and renew policies to all individuals and may not discriminate based on health status.

Beginning in 2014, most U.S. citizens and legal residents will be required to have insurance or pay a penalty. In its June 28, 2012, decision, the Supreme Court ruled that ACA's individual insurance mandate is within Congress's constitutional power to levy taxes (see earlier text box). As plans will no longer be able to restrict coverage of individuals with health problems, the individual mandate is intended to ensure that healthy individuals participate in the insurance market rather than waiting until they need health care services. Increasing the number of healthy persons in the risk pool helps spread the risk.

ACA requires employers with more than 200 full-time employees that offer health insurance benefits to automatically enroll new employees in a coverage plan, though employees must be given adequate notice and the opportunity to opt out. Employers with 50 or more full-time employees that have at least one employee who is enrolled in an exchange plan and receiving a premium tax credit may be subject to penalties, whether or not they provide health insurance coverage to their employees.[12]

As already noted, ACA requires state Medicaid programs to expand coverage to all nonelderly, non-pregnant legal residents with incomes up to 133% of FPL. Under the Supreme Court's decision, however, states may now choose whether to expand their Medicaid programs without fear of penalty. Several states have announced that they plan to opt out of the Medicaid expansion. States making that decision would forgo a substantial amount of federal funding. The federal government will provide 100% of the costs of the expansion for the first three years, phasing down to 90% in the years thereafter. Moreover, if a state decides not to expand its Medicaid program, low-income adults below the poverty line (i.e., below 100% FPL) who were not covered by, or eligible for, the state's existing Medicaid program, and who were seeking instead to purchase insurance coverage through an exchange (in accordance with the individual insurance mandate), would in general be ineligible for the subsidies.[13]

---

[12] For more details on the employer penalties, see CRS Report R41159, *Summary of Potential Employer Penalties Under the Patient Protection and Affordable Care Act (PPACA)*, by Janemarie Mulvey.

[13] ACA exempts the following individuals from the individual mandate penalty: (1) those for whom the lowest-cost available plan exceeds 8% of their income; (2) those with incomes below the tax filing threshold; (3) those without coverage for less than three months; and (4) members of an Indian tribe. Thus, most low-income individuals residing in states that choose not to expand their Medicaid programs would not be penalized for failing to purchase insurance coverage through an exchange. ACA also gives the HHS Secretary the authority to establish a hardship exemption. In a July 10, 2012, letter to state governors, Secretary Sebelius indicated that she intended to exercise that authority as appropriate to exempt low-income individuals who would not qualify for one of the four statutory exemptions.

Finally, ACA requires states to maintain the current CHIP structure through FY2019, and extends CHIP appropriations through FY2015.[14]

Estimated Budgetary Impact

At the time of ACA's enactment in March 2010, CBO and the Joint Committee on Taxation (JCT) estimated that the law's provisions to expand insurance coverage would result in gross costs of $938 billion over the 10-year period FY2010-FY2019. Gross costs include the exchange subsidies and related spending, increased spending on Medicaid and CHIP, and tax credits for certain small employers. CBO and JCT further estimated that those costs would be partially offset by an estimated $150 billion from penalties paid by uninsured individuals and employers, an excise tax on high-premium insurance plans, and net savings from other effects that coverage expansion is expected to have on tax revenues and outlays. Thus, CBO and JCT projected in their March 2010 baseline budget projections that ACA's insurance coverage provisions would result in net costs of $788 billion (i.e., $938 billion-$150 billion) over the FY2010-FY2019 period.[15]

The net costs of coverage expansion under ACA are further offset by (1) new revenues from taxes and fees (other than those related to insurance coverage, mentioned above); and (2) direct spending savings from payment and delivery system reform provisions that are designed to slow the rate of growth of Medicare spending and improve outcomes and the quality of care. In the March 2010 baseline, CBO and JCT projected that the new revenues and direct spending savings—briefly described in separate sections below—would total $912 billion over the 10-year period FY2010-FY2019. Based on those projections, CBO and JCT estimated overall that ACA implementation would reduce federal deficits by $124 billion over that period.[16]

CBO and JCT have updated their estimates of ACA's impact on federal direct spending and revenues several times since March 2010. The most recent estimates were released in July 2012. They take into account the Supreme Court's decision in *National Federation of Independent Business v. Sebelius*, which precludes the Secretary from penalizing states that choose not to participate in the Medicaid expansion. **Table 1** summarizes all five CBO and JCT estimates of ACA's impact on the federal deficit. Note that the three most recent estimates include only the gross and net costs of insurance coverage expansion. They do not include updated projections of the law's other offsetting revenues and direct spending savings.

CBO and JCT's estimates of the gross and net costs of expanding insurance coverage have grown significantly over time. For example, net costs increased from $788 billion in the March 2010 estimates to $1,252 billion in the March 2012 estimates (see **Table 1**). The difference is due in part to changes in the timing and/or length of the budget window. The 2010 and 2011 estimates both use a 10-year budget window. However, the 2010 estimates cover the period FY2010-FY2019, whereas the 2011 estimates begin and end two years later—FY2012-FY2021—and thus capture an additional two years of spending on exchange subsidies and Medicaid expansion. The

---

[14] For more details on ACA's changes to the Medicaid and CHIP programs, see CRS Report R41210, *Medicaid and the State Children's Health Insurance Program (CHIP) Provisions in ACA: Summary and Timeline*, by Evelyne P. Baumrucker et al.

[15] U.S. Congressional Budget Office, letter to the Honorable Nancy Pelosi, Speaker, U.S. House of Representatives, providing an estimate of the direct spending and revenue effects of ACA, as amended by HCERA (March 20, 2010), http://www.cbo.gov/sites/default/files/cbofiles/ftpdocs/113xx/doc11379/amendreconprop.pdf. See Table 4.

[16] Ibid. See Table 1.

March 2012 estimates also begin in FY2012 but cover an 11-year period (i.e., FY2012-FY2022). Other factors influencing the ACA budgetary estimates include (1) changes in the economic outlook, (2) enactment of legislation that modified ACA's insurance coverage provisions, (3) reduced growth in private health care spending, and (4) technical changes in the estimating procedures used by CBO and JCT.

Table 1. Impact of ACA on the Federal Deficit

Dollars in Billions

	Mar. 2010 Estimates (2010-2019)	Feb. 2011 Estimates (2012-2021)	Mar. 2011 Estimates (2012-2021)	Mar. 2012 Estimates (2012-2022)	July 2012 Estimates: Supreme Ct. Decision (2012-2022)
Insurance Coverage Expansion					
Gross cost	938	1,390	1,445	1,762	1,683
Medicaid and CHIP (non-add)	434	n.a.	627	931	642
Exchange subsidies (non-add)	464	n.a.	777	808	1,017
Employer tax credit (non-add)	40	n.a.	41	23	23
Net cost	788	1,042	1,131	1,252	1,168
Other direct spending	-492	-732	n.a.	n.a.	n.a.
Other revenues	-420	-520	n.a.	n.a.	n.a.
Net Impact on Federal Deficit	**-124**	**-210**	**n.a.**	**n.a.**	**n.a.**

Sources: (1) Estimates for March 2010, and February and March 2011: U.S. Congress, House Committee on Energy and Commerce, Subcommittee on Health, "CBO's Analysis of the Major Health Care Legislation Enacted in March 2010," Statement of Douglas W. Elmendorf, Director, 112th Cong., 1st sess., March 30, 2011, http://www.cbo.gov/ftpdocs/121xx/doc12119/03-30-HealthCareLegislation.pdf. See Tables 1 and 2. (2) Estimates for March and July 2012: U.S. Congressional Budget Office, "Estimates for the Insurance Coverage Provisions of the Affordable Care Act Updated for the Recent Supreme Court Decision," July 24, 2012, http://www.cbo.gov/sites/default/files/cbofiles/attachments/43472-07-24-2012-CoverageEstimates.pdf. See Table 2.

Notes: Numbers may not add up to totals due to rounding; n.a. = not available.

ACA, as enacted, requires each state to expand its Medicaid program by 2014 or risk losing federal matching funds for the existing program. CBO and JCT's budgetary estimates prior to the Supreme Court's decision assumed that every state would expand eligibility for coverage under its Medicaid program as specified in ACA. In the July 2012 estimates, which reflect the Court's decision, CBO and JCT anticipate that some states will opt out of the Medicaid expansion altogether while others will only partially expand their Medicaid programs. CBO and JCT also assume that some states will delay Medicaid expansion until some time after 2014.

As shown in **Table 1**, CBO and JCT now estimate that the insurance coverage provisions in ACA will have a net cost of $1,168 billion over the 11-year period FY2012-FY2022. That represents a decrease of $84 billion from the March 2012 estimate of $1,252 billion over the same period. These projected savings arise largely because the estimated reduction in spending as a result of lower Medicaid enrollment more than offsets the estimated increase in subsidies due to higher enrollment in the exchanges. Federal spending for Medicaid and CHIP is now projected to be $642 billion for the period FY2012-FY2022, which is $289 billion less than previously estimated, whereas the estimated cost of the exchange subsidies is now $1,017 billion for the same period, which represents an increase of $210 billion over the March 2012 estimate.

Estimated Impact on Insurance Coverage

Table 2 shows CBO and JCT's estimates of the impact of ACA implementation on insurance coverage among legal nonelderly U.S. residents. In the March 2012 baseline, prior to the Supreme Court's decision, CBO and JCT estimated that ACA would increase the number of nonelderly Americans with health insurance by about 33 million in 2022. Expansion of the Medicaid and CHIP programs was expected to enroll 17 million additional individuals in 2022, accounting for roughly half of the increase in coverage. The other half was due to a projected increase in private health insurance coverage. An estimated 22 million people were expected to purchase their own coverage through insurance exchanges in 2022. However, about 6 million fewer people were projected to obtain coverage through their employers or purchase individual coverage directly from insurers, resulting in an estimated net increase in the number of people with private insurance coverage of about 16 million.

Following the Supreme Court decision, CBO and JCT now estimate that fewer people will be covered by the Medicaid program, more people will obtain health insurance through the exchanges, and more people will remain uninsured. The July 2012 baseline projects that in 2022 an additional 11 million people will be covered by Medicaid and CHIP, which is 6 million fewer people than previously estimated, and about 25 million people will be enrolled in exchanges, which is 3 million more people than the earlier estimate. Overall, CBO and JCT estimate that about 3 million fewer people will gain health insurance coverage in 2022 as a result of the Supreme Court decision (see **Table 2**).

Table 2. Impact of ACA on Health Insurance Coverage

Millions of Nonelderly People

	Change in Coverage by 2022	
	March 2012 Estimates	**July 2012 Estimates: Supreme Ct. Decision**
Medicaid and CHIP	17	11
Employment-based coverage[a]	-3	-4
Nongroup and other[b]	-3	-3
Exchanges	22	25
Total	**33**	**30**

Source: U.S. Congressional Budget Office, "Estimates for the Insurance Coverage Provisions of the Affordable Care Act Updated for the Recent Supreme Court Decision," July 24, 2012, http://www.cbo.gov/sites/default/files/cbofiles/attachments/43472-07-24-2012-CoverageEstimates.pdf. See Table 1.

Notes: Numbers may not add to totals due to rounding.

a. The change in employer-based coverage is the net result of increases in and loss of such coverage.

b. Other includes Medicare; however, the effects of ACA are almost entirely on nongroup (i.e., individual) coverage.

Revenues

The increase in revenues is achieved largely by raising taxes on high-income households and by imposing fees on insurers and on manufacturers and importers of pharmaceuticals and medical devices.[17] In the February 2011 baseline, CBO and JCT estimated that those revenues would total $520 billion over the 10-year period FY2012-FY2021 (see **Table 1**).

Savings from Payment and Delivery System Reforms

ACA included numerous Medicare payment provisions intended to reduce the rate of growth in spending. They include reductions in Medicare Advantage (MA) plan payments and a lowering of the annual payment update for hospitals and certain other providers.[18] ACA established an Independent Payment Advisory Board (IPAB) to make recommendations for achieving specific Medicare spending reductions if costs exceed a target growth rate. IPAB's recommendations will take effect unless Congress overrides them, in which case Congress would be responsible for achieving the same level of savings.[19] Also, ACA provided tools to help reduce fraud, waste, and abuse in both Medicare and Medicaid.

Other provisions establish pilot, demonstration, and grant programs to test integrated models of care, including accountable care organizations (ACOs), medical homes that provide coordinated care for high-need individuals, and bundling payments for acute-care episodes (including hospitalization and follow-up care). ACA created the Center for Medicare and Medicaid Innovation (CMMI) to pilot payment and service delivery models, primarily for Medicare and Medicaid beneficiaries. The law also established new pay-for-reporting and pay-for-performance programs within Medicare that will pay providers based on the reporting of, or performance on, selected quality measures.

Additionally, ACA created incentives for promoting primary care and prevention; for example, by increasing primary care payment rates under Medicare and Medicaid, covering recommended preventive services without cost-sharing, and funding community-based prevention and employer wellness programs, among other things. The law increased funding for community health centers and the National Health Service Corps to expand access to primary care services in rural and medically underserved areas and reduce health disparities. Finally, ACA required the HHS Secretary to develop a national strategy for health care quality to improve care delivery, patient outcomes, and population health.

In the February 2011 baseline, CBO and JCT estimated that the health care payment and delivery system reform provisions in ACA would result overall in a net reduction in direct health care spending of $732 billion over the period FY2012-FY2021 (see **Table 1**).

---

[17] For more information about the revenue provisions in ACA, see CRS Report R41128, *Health-Related Revenue Provisions in the Patient Protection and Affordable Care Act (ACA)*, by Janemarie Mulvey.

[18] For more information about the Medicare provisions in ACA, see CRS Report R41196, *Medicare Provisions in the Patient Protection and Affordable Care Act (PPACA): Summary and Timeline*, coordinated by Patricia A. Davis.

[19] For more information about IPAB, see CRS Report R41511, *The Independent Payment Advisory Board*, by Jim Hahn and Christopher M. Davis.

Impact of Automatic Spending Reductions on Health Reform Spending

As noted in the introduction to this report, the BCA instructed the Joint Committee to develop legislation that would reduce the federal budget deficit by a total of at least $1.5 trillion over the period FY2012-FY2021. If Joint Committee legislation estimated to produce more than $1.2 trillion in deficit reduction were not enacted by January 15, 2012, then automatic procedures for cutting both discretionary and direct (i.e., mandatory) spending would take effect beginning in FY2013. The November 21, 2011, announcement by the Joint Committee that it was unable to agree on deficit-reduction legislation means that automatic spending reductions totaling $1.2 trillion (including an allowance for reduced interest payments on the debt) are all but certain to take effect, unless Congress and the President enact legislation to modify or repeal the BCA.

Based on the formula in the BCA, the automatic spending reductions would cut the same amount—$54.7 billion—from both defense and nondefense spending for each fiscal year over the period FY2013-FY2021. The annual spending cuts in each category—defense and nondefense—would be divided proportionately between discretionary and nonexempt direct spending. Direct spending reductions would be executed each year through a sequestration (i.e., an across-the-board cancellation) of budgetary resources in nonexempt accounts.

The sequestration process was first established in 1985 by the Balanced Budget and Emergency Deficit Control Act (BBEDCA), commonly known as the Gramm-Rudman-Hollings Act.[20] Initially, sequestration was tied to annual maximum deficit targets. If the budget deficit exceeded those target levels, then automatic across-the-board spending cuts would be triggered. The BBEDCA has been amended several times, notably by the Budget Enforcement Act of 1990,[21] which tied sequestration to new statutory spending limits, and most recently by the BCA. The sequestration process is subject to exemptions and to certain rules, which are specified in sections 255 and 256, respectively, of the BBEDCA.[22] Several of those provisions relate to health spending under ACA and are discussed below.

Under the sequestration rules, reductions in Medicare payments to health care providers and health plans (which account for most of Medicare spending) are capped at 2%. Many other federal direct spending programs, accounting for most of the government's entitlement and other direct spending (excluding Medicare), are exempt from sequestration altogether.[23]

Discretionary spending reductions in FY2013 also would be achieved through a sequestration of nonexempt discretionary appropriations. The sequestration rules exempt some discretionary spending, notably for veterans' health care and Pell grants.[24] For each of the remaining fiscal years (i.e., FY2014-FY2021), however, discretionary spending reductions would be achieved by

---

[20] P.L. 99-177, Title II, 99 Stat. 1038.

[21] P.L. 101-508, Title XIII, 104 Stat. 1388-573.

[22] For an overview of the BBEDCA exemptions and special rules, see CRS Report R42050, *Budget "Sequestration" and Selected Program Exemptions and Special Rules*, coordinated by Karen Spar.

[23] Ibid.

[24] Ibid. Note: All veterans programs, mandatory and discretionary, are exempt from sequestration.

lowering the BCA discretionary spending caps.[25] There would be no across-the-board cuts through sequestration. Instead, the Appropriations Committees would decide how to apportion the cuts within the reduced cap.

The BCA requires the Office of Management and Budget (OMB) to calculate, and the President to order, the sequestration of nonexempt discretionary appropriations for FY2013 and nonexempt direct spending for each of FY2013 through FY2021. The sequestration for FY2013 is to occur on January 2, 2013, and the sequestration for each subsequent fiscal year is to occur at the time of the President's annual budget submission in early February.

On September 14, OMB released a report on the potential impact of a sequestration triggered by the failure of the Joint Committee to propose, and Congress and the President to enact, legislation to reduce the deficit by an amount greater than $1.2 trillion.[26] The OMB report provides a breakdown of exempt and nonexempt budget accounts, and includes estimates of the FY2013 funding reductions in nonexempt accounts.

Table 3 summarizes OMB's estimates for *nondefense* spending. OMB calculated that sequestration would result in an 8.2% reduction in nonexempt discretionary spending and a 7.6% reduction in spending under nonexempt mandatory programs. Sequestration also would impose cuts of 2% on (1) Medicare payments to health plans and health care providers and (2) mandatory spending on health centers and Indian health. OMB emphasized that the estimates and budget account classifications in the report are preliminary. The agency noted that "[i]f the sequestration were to occur, the actual results would differ based on changes in law and ongoing legal, budgetary, and technical analysis."[27]

Table 3. Impact of Sequestration on FY2013 Nondefense Spending

OMB's Preliminary Estimates, Sept. 2012

Programs	Percent Reduction
Discretionary Spending	
Nonexempt programs	8.2%
Direct (Mandatory) Spending	
Medicare payments to providers and plans	2.0%
Health centers and Indian health	2.0%
Nonexempt programs	7.6%

Source: Office of Management and Budget.

---

[25] As already noted (see footnote 8), the annual discretionary spending caps for FY2012-FY2021 would be revised if automatic spending reductions were triggered. The overall discretionary spending limit for each fiscal year would remain unchanged, but that amount would be divided between defense discretionary spending and all other (i.e., nondefense) discretionary spending. Discretionary spending reductions, whether by sequestration (FY2013) or through a downward adjustment of the revised spending caps (FY2014-FY2021), would be applied to both defense and nondefense spending categories.

[26] U.S. Office of Management and Budget, *OMB Report Pursuant to the Sequestration Transparency Act of 2012 (P.L. 112-155)*, http://www.whitehouse.gov/sites/default/files/omb/assets/legislative_reports/stareport.pdf.

[27] Ibid., p. 1.

The remaining sections of this report discuss the potential impact of a Joint Committee sequestration on ACA FY2013 spending in the following areas: (1) insurance coverage expansion, including exchanges subsidies and Medicaid; (2) other mandatory spending; (3) discretionary spending; and (4) federal administrative costs.

Insurance Coverage Expansion

It appears that most of ACA's projected spending on expanding insurance coverage would not be subject to sequestration in the event that spending reductions are triggered under the BCA. First, the BBEDCA exempts the Medicaid and CHIP programs from sequestration.[28] According to CBO and JCT's July 2012 estimates, Medicaid and CHIP outlays are projected to account for $642 billion, or 38%, of the gross costs of $1,683 billion for coverage expansion over the FY2012-FY2022 period (see **Table 4**).[29]

Second, the refundable tax credits available to individuals and families with incomes between 100% and 400% of the FPL for purchasing insurance coverage through the exchanges also would likely be exempt from a sequestration order. While the ACA premium tax credits are not specifically exempted from sequestration, the BBEDCA provides a general exemption for refundable individual tax credits.[30] These premium tax credits have the effect of limiting the cost of purchasing coverage to a specified percentage of income. Based on CBO and JCT's July 2012 estimates, the premium tax credits account for approximately $854 billion, or 84%, of ACA's total exchange subsidies and related spending of $1,017 billion over the FY2012-FY2022 period (see **Table 4**), which itself represents about 60% of the $1,683 billion in gross costs for coverage expansion.[31]

In addition to the premium tax credits for purchasing coverage through an exchange, certain individuals and families receiving the credits are also eligible for coverage with lower cost-sharing (i.e., out-of-pocket costs such as deductibles and co-pays) than otherwise required under the law. This is achieved through a cost-sharing subsidy, which is paid directly to the insurer to cover the extra costs associated with lower patient cost-sharing. In the absence of any applicable exemption under BBEDCA, mandatory spending on the cost-sharing subsidies would presumably be fully sequestrable at a rate of 7.6%, according to OMB's preliminary analysis.[32] Based on

---

[28] Low-income programs, including Medicaid and CHIP, that are exempt from sequestration are listed in BBEDCA Section 255(h). 2 U.S.C. §905(h).

[29] U.S. Congressional Budget Office, "Estimates for the Insurance Coverage Provisions of the Affordable Care Act Updated for the Recent Supreme Court Decision," July 24, 2012, http://www.cbo.gov/sites/default/files/cbofiles/attachments/43472-07-24-2012-CoverageEstimates.pdf. See Table 2.

[30] BBEDCA Section 255(d) reads as follows: "Payments to individuals made pursuant to provisions of the Internal Revenue Code of 1986 establishing refundable tax credits shall be exempt from reduction under any order issued under this part." 2 U.S.C. §905(d).

[31] U.S. Congressional Budget Office, "Estimates for the Insurance Coverage Provisions of the Affordable Care Act Updated for the Recent Supreme Court Decision," July 24, 2012, http://www.cbo.gov/sites/default/files/cbofiles/attachments/43472-07-24-2012-CoverageEstimates.pdf. See Table 2. Note: The estimated share of premium tax credit spending as a percentage of ACA's total exchange subsidies and related spending is based on the figures provided in CBO's March 2012 baseline at http://www.cbo.gov/sites/default/files/cbofiles/attachments/43057_HealthInsuranceExchanges.pdf.

[32] The impact of such an order is unclear. ACA entitles certain low-income exchange enrollees to coverage with reduced cost-sharing and requires the participating insurers to provide that coverage. Sequestration would not change that requirement. In the event of a sequestration order, insurers presumably would still have to provide required coverage to qualifying enrollees but they would not receive the full subsidy to cover their increased costs.

CBO and JCT's July 2012 estimates, the cost-sharing subsidies account for an additional $152 billion, or 15%, of ACA's total exchange subsidies and related spending over the FY2012-FY2022 period (see **Table 4**).[33]

Finally, mandatory spending on the small employer tax credits to help offset the cost of purchasing health insurance for their employees also would presumably be subject to sequestration at OMB's estimated rate of 7.6%.[34] These credits are available to for-profit and nonprofit employers with fewer than 25 FTEs and average annual wages of less than $50,000.[35] According to CBO and JCT's July 2012 estimate, the small employer tax credits are projected to cost $23 billion over the FY2012-FY2022 period, or about 1% of the $1,683 billion in gross costs for coverage expansion (see **Table 4**).[36]

Other Mandatory Spending

ACA included numerous mandatory appropriations that provide billions of dollars to support new and existing grant programs and other activities. Many of the provisions are annual appropriations of specified amounts for one or more fiscal years. A few of them are multiple-year appropriations, in which the amount appropriated is available for obligation for a definite period of time in excess of one fiscal year (e.g., for the period FY2011-FY2014). Often the provision includes additional language stating that the funds are to remain available "until expended" or "without fiscal year limitation."

ACA appropriated billions of dollars for temporary programs for targeted groups, including (1) $5 billion for the Pre-Existing Condition Insurance Plan (PCIP), a temporary insurance program to provide health insurance coverage for uninsured individuals with a preexisting condition; (2) $5 billion for a temporary reinsurance program to reimburse employers for a portion of the costs of providing health benefits to early retirees aged 55-64; and (3) $6 billion for the Consumer Operated and Oriented Plan (CO-OP) program, to establish temporary health insurance cooperatives.[37] ACA also included money for states to plan and establish health insurance exchanges. The law provided $10 billion for the FY2011-FY2019 period—and $10 billion for each subsequent 10-year period—for the CMMI to test and implement innovative payment and

---

[33] U.S. Congressional Budget Office, "Estimates for the Insurance Coverage Provisions of the Affordable Care Act Updated for the Recent Supreme Court Decision," July 24, 2012. Available at http://www.cbo.gov/sites/default/files/cbofiles/attachments/43472-07-24-2012-CoverageEstimates.pdf. See Table 2. Note: The estimated share of the cost-sharing subsidies as a percentage of ACA's total exchange subsidies and related spending is based on the figures provided in CBO's March 2012 baseline, available at http://www.cbo.gov/sites/default/files/cbofiles/attachments/43057_HealthInsuranceExchanges.pdf.

[34] Among the programs and activities listed as being exempt from a sequestration order, BBEDCA Section 255 includes payments to individuals in the form of refundable tax credits (see footnote 30). It does not include small employer tax credits.

[35] For more details on the small employer tax credit, see CRS Report R41158, *Summary of Small Business Health Insurance Tax Credit Under the Patient Protection and Affordable Care Act (ACA)*, by Janemarie Mulvey and Hinda Chaikind.

[36] U.S. Congressional Budget Office, "Estimates for the Insurance Coverage Provisions of the Affordable Care Act Updated for the Recent Supreme Court Decision," July 24, 2012, http://www.cbo.gov/sites/default/files/cbofiles/attachments/43472-07-24-2012-CoverageEstimates.pdf. See Table 2.

[37] Section 1857 of the Department of Defense and Full-Year Continuing Appropriations Act, 2011 (P.L. 112-10, 125 Stat. 38) canceled $2.2 billion of the $6 billion appropriation for the CO-OP program. Section 524 in Division F of the Consolidated Appropriations Act, 2012 (P.L. 112-74, 125 Stat. 786) rescinded an additional $400 million from the CO-OP appropriation.

---

service delivery models, and it funded an independent board (i.e., IPAB) to provide Congress with proposals for reducing Medicare cost growth and improving quality of care for Medicare beneficiaries.

ACA created four special funds and appropriated substantial amounts to each. First, the Community Health Center Fund (CHCF) will provide a total of $11 billion in annual appropriations over five years (FY2011-FY2015) in supplemental funding for community health center operations and the National Health Service Corps. (A separate ACA appropriation provided $1.5 billion for health center construction and renovation.) Second, the Patient-Centered Outcomes Research Trust Fund (PCORTF) will support comparative effectiveness research through FY2019 with a mix of annual appropriations and transfers from the Medicare trust funds. Third, the Prevention and Public Health Fund (PPHF), for which ACA provided a permanent annual appropriation, is intended to support prevention, wellness, and other public health-related programs and activities authorized under the Public Health Service Act (PHSA).[38] Finally, ACA provided $1 billion to the Health Insurance Reform Implementation Fund (HIRIF) to help cover the administrative costs of implementing the law.

In addition, ACA appropriated $2.4 billion for maternal and child health programs. Overall, the law included more than $100 billion in direct appropriations over the 10-year period FY2010-FY2019, including $40 billion to provide two more years of funding for CHIP (see **Table 4**).[39]

A few of the appropriations in ACA are included in CBO and JCT's estimate of the costs of coverage expansion (e.g., PCIP, CO-OP, exchange establishment grants). All the remaining amounts—including funding for community health centers, health workforce programs, and public health activities—are captured in CBO's overall estimate of the impact of the law's payment and delivery system reform provisions on direct spending.

The mandatory appropriations in ACA would, in general, be subject to OMB's estimated 7.6% reduction under a sequestration order. However, for any given fiscal year in which sequestration was ordered, only new budget authority for that year (including advance appropriations that first become available for obligation in that year) would be reduced. Unobligated balances (non-defense only) carried over from previous fiscal years are exempt from a sequestration order.[40] Thus, an FY2013 sequestration order to reduce direct spending would not apply to unobligated ACA funds that had been appropriated in a prior fiscal year (i.e., FY2010-FY2012) and were still available for obligation.

The exemption for unobligated balances carried over from prior fiscal years is a potentially important one that would apply to a number of ACA appropriations. As already mentioned, the appropriation provision often specifies that the funds are to remain available "until expended" or "without fiscal year limitation." One example is the PCIP program to provide health insurance coverage for eligible individuals who have been uninsured for six months and have a preexisting

---

[38] Section 3205 of the Middle Class Tax Relief and Job Creation Act of 2012 (P.L. 112-96) reduced ACA's appropriations to the PPHF over the period FY2013-FY2021 by a total of $6.25 billion. Under ACA, the PPHF would have received a total of $16.75 billion over that nine-year period; P.L. 112-96 reduced that amount to $10.50 billion.

[39] For more details on all of ACA's mandatory appropriations, see CRS Report R41301, *Appropriations and Fund Transfers in the Patient Protection and Affordable Care Act (PPACA)*, by C. Stephen Redhead.

[40] An exemption for non-defense unobligated balances is provided in BBEDCA Section 255(e). It reads as follows: "Unobligated balances of budget authority carried over from prior fiscal years, except balances in the defense category, shall be exempt from reduction under any order issued under this part." 2 U.S.C. §905(e).

---

condition. The program terminates on January 1, 2014. ACA appropriated $5 billion in FY2010, to remain available without fiscal year limitation, to pay claims against the PCIP that are in excess of the premiums collected from enrollees. Any unobligated PCIP funds in FY2013 would be exempt from sequestration.[41]

According to OMB's preliminary analysis, the FY2013 appropriations for both PPHF and PCORTF would be fully sequestrable at the 7.6% rate applicable to direct (i.e., mandatory) spending. However, for reasons discussed below, sequestration of ACA's FY2013 appropriation to the CHCF would be capped at 2%.

Discretionary Spending

ACA implementation will affect not only direct spending and revenues but also discretionary spending, which is provided in and controlled by annual appropriations acts. The law reauthorized appropriations for numerous existing discretionary grant programs and activities authorized under the PHSA, and permanently reauthorized appropriations for programs and services provided by the Indian Health Service (IHS). While the authorizations of appropriations for most programs had expired prior to their reauthorization in ACA, most of them continued to receive an annual appropriation. ACA also created a number of new grant programs and provided for each an authorization of appropriations.[42]

Many of ACA's discretionary spending provisions authorized annual appropriations of specified amounts for one or more fiscal years. Other provisions authorized the appropriation of specified amounts for FY2010 or FY2011 and unspecified amounts—such sums as may be necessary, or SSAN—for later years. A few provisions authorized multi-year appropriations, available for obligation for a period in excess of one fiscal year. Numerous other provisions simply authorized the appropriation of SSAN, in a few cases without specifying any fiscal years.

Funding for all these discretionary programs depends on actions taken by congressional appropriators, a process that may lead to greater or smaller amounts than the sums authorized by ACA. With Congress now operating under BCA's discretionary spending limits, it may prove difficult to secure funding for new programs and activities. To date, few new discretionary programs authorized by ACA have received funding through the annual appropriations process, though a handful have received funding from the PPHF.[43] Even maintaining current funding levels for existing programs with an established appropriations history may prove a challenge under growing pressure to reduce federal discretionary spending.

CBO estimated that ACA's discretionary spending provisions, if fully funded by future appropriations acts, would result in appropriations of almost $100 billion over the period FY2012-FY2021 (see **Table 4**).[44] However, most of that funding—about $85 billion—would be

---

[41] Table 2 in CRS Report R41301, *Appropriations and Fund Transfers in the Patient Protection and Affordable Care Act (PPACA)*, shows all the ACA appropriations by fiscal year over the period FY2010-FY2019 and, for each provision, indicates whether the funds are to remain available for an indefinite period of time (i.e., until expended, or without fiscal year limitation), subject to any requirement that the program terminate on a specific date.

[42] For more details on all of ACA's discretionary spending provisions, see CRS Report R41390, *Discretionary Spending in the Patient Protection and Affordable Care Act (ACA)*, coordinated by C. Stephen Redhead.

[43] Ibid.

[44] U.S. Congress, House Committee on Energy and Commerce, Subcommittee on Health, "CBO's Analysis of the (continued...)

---

for programs that were in existence prior to, and were reauthorized by, ACA; namely, the National Health Service Corps, the health centers program, and the IHS.

In general, ACA-related discretionary spending in FY2013 would be fully sequestrable at the 8.2% rate, according to OMB's preliminary analysis. Importantly, OMB concluded that the sequestration rules under BBEDCA section 256, which include a 2% limit on cuts in spending on health centers and the IHS, would apply only to mandatory spending reductions and not to cuts in discretionary spending. Thus, FY2013 discretionary spending on health centers would be subject to an 8.2% sequestration, whereas cuts in CHCF (mandatory) funding for health centers would be capped at 2%.[45]

For each of the remaining years (i.e., FY2014-FY2021), discretionary spending reductions would be achieved through a downward adjustment of the revised statutory spending limits. In contrast to the automatic spending reductions achieved through sequestration, lowering the annual discretionary spending limits allows Congress and the President to determine through the annual appropriations process which accounts are to be reduced, and by how much, in order to meet those limits.[46] Lowering the annual spending limits also would make it that much more of a challenge to maintain funding levels for existing programs.

Federal Administrative Expenses

CBO has projected that both HHS and the Internal Revenue Service (IRS) will incur substantial administrative costs to implement the policies and programs established by ACA. CBO estimated that the costs to the IRS of implementing the eligibility determination, documentation, and verification processes for premium and cost-sharing subsidies will probably total between $5 billion and $10 billion over 10 years. It further estimated that the costs to HHS for implementing

---

(...continued)

Major Health Care Legislation Enacted in March 2010," Statement of Douglas W. Elmendorf, Director, 112th Cong., 1st sess., March 30, 2011. Available at http://www.cbo.gov/ftpdocs/121xx/doc12119/03-30-HealthCareLegislation.pdf. See p. 16. CBO's estimate of discretionary spending includes (1) amounts specified in ACA, plus estimated amounts for subsequent years (adjusted for anticipated inflation) where ACA specified an amount for the first year and authorized SSAN for subsequent years; and (2) estimated amounts for subsequent years (adjusted for anticipated inflation) where there was an appropriation under existing law for FY2010, and ACA authorized the appropriation of SSAN for later years. The CBO estimate does not include new ACA programs for which the law provided only an authorization for the appropriation of SSAN.

[45] Based on its statutory interpretation of BBEDCA, OMB determined that a Joint Committee sequestration would not be implemented as an order issued under BBEDCA section 254, as are sequestration orders to enforce the discretionary spending limits (BBEDCA section 251) and the pay-as-you-go, or PAYGO, requirements (BBEDCA section 252). This is significant because the section 256 rules apply only to a sequestration order issued under section 254. Thus, OMB concluded that the section 256 rules "do not apply to a Joint Committee sequestration, except to the extent those rules are otherwise made applicable by another provision of law." While section 251A(8) of BBEDCA specifically applies the section 256 rules to a Joint Committee sequestration of nonexempt direct spending, there is no such provision for discretionary spending in section 251A(7).

[46] The revised discretionary spending limits for FY2014-FY2021 would be enforced through a separate sequestration process pursuant to BBEDCA section 251 (see previous footnote). If discretionary appropriations within either category (i.e., defense or nondefense) exceeded the spending limit for that category, then across-the-board cuts would be triggered in nonexempt discretionary appropriation accounts, within the category in which the breach occurred, by an amount necessary to eliminate the breach.

---

the changes in Medicare, Medicaid, and CHIP, as well as some of the reforms to the private insurance market, will require similar amounts over 10 years.[47]

In general, under BBEDCA section 256, federal administrative expenses are subject to sequestration, regardless of whether they are incurred in connection with a program or activity that is otherwise exempt or subject to a special rule.[48] Thus, while the ACA refundable tax credits may be exempt from sequestration, the federal administrative expenses associated with the program would be sequestrable. Section 256 provides an exception for federal payments to state and local governments that match or reimburse these governments for their own administrative costs. Such payments are not considered federal administrative expenses and are subject to sequestration, but only to the extent that the relevant federal program is subject to sequestration.[49] For example, federal payments to state Medicaid programs for administrative costs would be exempt from sequestration because the Medicaid program as a whole is exempt.

However, as discussed in the previous section, OMB has determined that the sequestration rules in BBEDCA section 256 would apply only to direct spending reductions required by a Joint Committee sequestration, and not to reductions in discretionary spending. With regard to federal administrative expenses, OMB concluded that mandatory administrative expenses for an otherwise exempt (i.e., non-sequestrable) program are subject to sequestration (pursuant to section 256), whereas discretionary administrative expenses for an otherwise exempt (i.e., non-sequestrable) program are not sequestrable.

It has already been noted that ACA provided $1 billion in mandatory funds to help cover the administrative costs of implementation. HHS projects that all those funds will have been obligated by the end of FY2012. Thereafter, ACA administrative costs will have to be funded by annual discretionary appropriations. The President's FY2013 budget requested more than $1 billion in new discretionary funding for HHS and the IRS to pay for ongoing administrative costs associated with ACA implementation. It remains unclear whether congressional appropriators will provide any or all of those funds in FY2013. Congress has yet to complete action on any of the FY2013 appropriations bills and has instead passed a continuing resolution, H.J.Res. 117, which provides temporary funding authority for the first six months of FY2013. The requested ACA administrative funding was not included in H.J.Res. 117.[50]

---

[47] U.S. Congress, House Committee on Energy and Commerce, Subcommittee on Health, "CBO's Analysis of the Major Health Care Legislation Enacted in March 2010," Statement of Douglas W. Elmendorf, Director, 112th Cong., 1st sess., March 30, 2011. Available at http://www.cbo.gov/ftpdocs/121xx/doc12119/03-30-HealthCareLegislation.pdf. See p. 15.

[48] BBEDCA Section 256(h)(1), 2 U.S.C. § 906(h)(1).

[49] BBEDCA Section 256(h)(3), 2 U.S.C. § 906(h)(3).

[50] H.J.Res. 117, the Continuing Appropriations Resolution, 2013, funds government operations at an annualized rate of $1.047 trillion in discretionary budget authority, which equals the FY2013 discretionary spending cap set by the BCA. It increases funding for most federal agencies and programs by 0.612% over the FY2012 levels. H.J.Res. 117 does not incorporate any of the new ACA-related policies or funding that were included in the President's FY2013 budget.

Table 4. Potential Impact of the Budget Control Act's Automatic Spending Reduction Procedures on Health Reform Spending

Type of Spending	Estimated Cost FY2012-FY2022 ($ billions)	Potential Impact of Spending Reductions
Insurance Coverage Expansion		
Medicaid/CHIP	$642	Medicaid and CHIP would both be exempt from a sequestration order.[a]
Exchange subsidies and related spending	$1,017	
Premium tax credit (non-add)	≈$854	Refundable tax credits available to individuals and families with incomes between 100% and 400% of the federal poverty level to offset the cost of purchasing insurance coverage through the exchanges would likely be exempt from a sequestration order.[b]
Cost-sharing subsidy (non-add)	≈$152	Cost-sharing subsidies available to certain individuals and families receiving the premium tax credit would presumably be subject to a sequestration order.
Small employer tax credit	$23	Tax credits available to certain small businesses and small tax-exempt organizations to offset the cost of covering their employees would presumably be subject to a sequestration order.[c]
Other Mandatory Spending	>$100[d]	Mandatory appropriations in ACA would, in general, be subject to direct spending reductions under a sequestration order. However, for any given fiscal year in which sequestration was ordered, only new budget authority for that year (including advance appropriations that first become available for obligation in that year) would be reduced. Unobligated balances carried over from previous fiscal years would be exempt from a sequestration order.[e] Sequestration of mandatory spending on health centers and the IHS would be capped at 2%. Note: the total includes $40 billion in advance appropriations for CHIP (FY2014-FY2015), which would be exempt from a sequestration order.
Discretionary Spending	≈$100[f]	ACA-related discretionary spending in FY2013 would, in general, be subject to a sequestration order. Spending reductions in later years (i.e., FY2014-FY2021) would be achieved through a downward adjustment of the revised discretionary spending limits.

Source: Table prepared by the Congressional Research Service based on CBO's July 2012 baseline budget projections for the Affordable Care Act's insurance coverage provisions.

a. Medicaid and CHIP are among the exempted low-income programs listed in BBEDCA Section 255(h).

b. While the ACA premium tax credits are not specifically exempted from sequestration, BBEDCA Section 255(d) provides a general exemption for refundable individual tax credits.

c. BBEDCA Section 255 does not include small employer tax credits among the list of programs and activities that are exempt from sequestration.

d. Note that this estimate refers to the 10-year period FY2010-FY2019. It is not possible to determine the total amount appropriated by ACA because several appropriations are for unspecified amounts (i.e., such sums as may be necessary) or contingent upon a formula or revenues from industry fees. For more details on all of ACA's mandatory appropriations, see CRS Report R41301, *Appropriations and Fund Transfers in the Patient Protection and Affordable Care Act (PPACA)*, by C. Stephen Redhead.

e. An exemption for non-defense unobligated balances is provided in BBEDCA Section 255(e).

f. This figure is CBO's estimate assuming that all ACA's discretionary spending provisions are fully funded by future appropriations acts. For more details on all of ACA's discretionary spending provisions, see CRS Report R41390, *Discretionary Spending in the Patient Protection and Affordable Care Act (ACA)*, coordinated by C. Stephen Redhead.

Author Contact Information

C. Stephen Redhead
Specialist in Health Policy
credhead@crs.loc.gov, 7-2261

www.ingramcontent.com/pod-product-compliance
Lightning Source LLC
Chambersburg PA
CBHW080803290526
45790CB00008B/3569